Pet Poems

Purrfect

AaaaA

When
you're
smitten by
a kitten, what's
your option?
One
adoption!

Liz Brownlee

If you enjoy *Pet Poems*, then why not try
Animal Poems, *School Poems* and *Magic Poems*,
also compiled by Jennifer Curry?

Pet
Poems

Compiled by
Jennifer Curry

Illustrated by
Sarah Nayler

■SCHOLASTIC

This book is for EMMA HATTERSLEY, a very special girl.

Scholastic Children's Books,
Commonwealth House, 1-19 New Oxford Street,
London, WC1A 1NU, UK
a division of Scholastic Ltd
London ~ New York ~ Toronto ~ Sydney ~ Auckland
Mexico City ~ New Delhi ~ Hong Kong

Published in the UK by Scholastic Ltd, 2001

ISBN 0 439 99359 8

Printed and bound in Great Britain by Cox & Wyman Ltd, Reading, Berks.

6 8 10 9 7 5

CONTENTS

Taster
Purrfect   Liz Brownlee   1

First Word
Pet Shop Rap   Coral Rumble   11

Haiku
When Lessons Get Dull   Jennifer Curry   13

Cool School Pets
Miss Flynn's Pangolin   Sue Cowling   14
The Fate of the School Hamster   Katie Dale   15
Me Memba Wen   Frederick Williams   16
Subtraction   Coral Rumble   17
Cool School Pets   Philip Waddell   18
Teacher's Pet   Tony Mitton   19

Haiku
Our Budgerigar   David Whitehead   21

My Iguana Loves Banana
Puppy and the Sausage   Gabriel Fitzmaurice   22
Dog Byte   Trevor Harvey   23
Stegosaurus   Wendy Larmont   25
My Pony   Sue Cowling   26
My Pet Alligator   Thomas Bull   27

Hello, How Are You? I Am Fine!   Jack Prelutsky   28
Iguana Rap   Moira Clark   30

Haiku

Sleeps, Eats, Plays, Eats   Mike Johnson   31

A Shaggy One Would Do

Poem Left Hopefully Lying Around Before
    Christmas   Eric Finney   32
The Invisible Man's Invisible Dog   Brian Patten   34
My Cocker Spaniel (Bonnie)   Joanne Brown   35
It's a Dog's Life   John Foster   36
War Dog   Ian Souter   38
Taking the (Shush) For a (Shush)   Daphne Phillips   40
Muffin – My Dog   Hayley Morris   41
My Dog, He is an Ugly dog   Jack Prelutsky   42

Haiku

Behind the Cupboard?   Ann Bonner   44

Gloomsday, Doomsday

Pet Palindrome   Eric Finney   45
Who's Seen Jip?   Wes Magee   46
Bad Design   Jez Alborough   47
The Cat Sat on the Computer   John Whitworth   48
Marmalade   Peter Dixon   50
The Great Gerbil Hunt   Judith Nicholls   52

Haiku

Peter Parrot Pecks   *Moira Clark* 53

Turkeys Jus Wanna Play Reggae

Quack, Quack!   *Dr Seuss* 54
My Parakeet   *Grace Nichols* 55
Talking Turkeys!   *Benjamin Zephaniah* 56
Barry's Budgie! Beware!   *David Harmer* 58
Sergeant Brown's Parrot   *Kit Wright* 59
Daddy-Long-Legs   *Judith Nicholls* 60

Haiku

Sad Eyes   *John Kitching* 61

Vet Required: Apply Within

At the Vet's   *Brian Moses* 62
At the Vet's   *Anne Allinson* 64
Dream Pet   *Sue Benwell* 65
Respect, Respect Your Cyberpet   *D J Ward* 66
Vet Required: Apply Within   *Bernard Young* 68
What Asana Wanted For Her Birthday *Grace Nichols* 70

Haiku

Glitter, My Goldfish   *Jenni Sinclair* 71

My Fish Can Ride a Bicycle

The Hopeful Frog   *Daphne Schiller* 72

Mary Had a Crocodile | Hilaire Belloc | 73
My Fish Can Ride a Bicycle | Jack Prelutsky | 74
Ode to a Goldfish | Gyles Brandreth | 75
Small Pet Poem | Mike Johnson | 76

Haiku

Don't Tell Anyone | Ann Bonner | 77

Whiskers Like Spiky Icicles

A Reasonable Rat | Laurelle Rond | 78
Pocket Friends | Mark Bones | 79
Who Am I? | John Kitching | 80
Rosie Super Rabbit | Alex Coburn | 81
My Rabbit | John Agard | 82
Have a Gerbil! | Ian Whybrow | 83
Our Cat's Thoughts... | Ian Whybrow | 84

Haiku

My Cat Has a Bell | Philip Burton | 85

My Cat's Groovy

I Had a Little Cat | Charles Causley | 86
My Cat | Nigel Gray | 87
Cat | Ann Bonner | 88
Animal Rights | Lindsay MacRae | 89
My Cat's Groovy | Gina Claye | 90
My Lovely Pussy Cat | Joanne Mathieson | 92

Haiku
My Cat Slinks   Jennifer Curry   93

What Shall We Call Him?
Our Dog Smartie   Ian Souter   94
Four Crazy Pets   Paul Cookson   96
A Parrot Called Mouse   Tim Pointon   98
What Shall We Call the Dog?   Eric Finney   99
Cat   Vernon Scannel   100

Haiku
Can You Believe It?   John Kitching   101

A Python in the Pantry
Wild Thing   Ann Bonner   102
Our Hippopotamus   Colin West   103
Ernie – the Great Collector   Patricia Leighton   104
My Stick Insect is Hiding   Coral Rumble   105
Our Car Pet   Philip Waddell   106
Luv Song   Benjamin Zephaniah   108
Pink Pet   Tim Pointon   109
The Yak   Hilaire Belloc   110
My Pet Mouse   David Whitehead   111
Guess the Pet   Philip Waddell   112
Auntie Babs   Colin West   114

Last Word
A Pet Is   Jane Whittle   115

PET SHOP

First Word

Pet Shop Rap

We've got a pet shop,
A noisy pet shop,
A chirping, barking pet shop,
We've got a pet shop,
A lively pet shop,
A splashing, dashing pet shop.

We've got …
Tiny gerbils
Purring cats
Cute little puppies
Black and white rats
Birds that sing
Mice that squeak
Hairy black spiders
Parrots that speak.

We've got a pet shop,
A noisy pet shop,
A chirping, barking pet shop,
We've got a pet shop,
A lively pet shop,
A splashing, dashing pet shop.

We've got …
Swimming turtles
Darting fish
Guinea pigs
Sitting in their dish
Hamsters that nibble
Snakes that glide
Rabbits that bounce
Lizards that hide.

We've got a pet shop,
A noisy pet shop,
A chirping, barking pet shop,
We've got a pet shop,
A lively pet shop,
A splashing, dashing pet shop.

Coral Rumble

Haiku

When lessons get dull
Leave the classroom behind and
Head for Pets Corner

Jennifer Curry

1, 2, 3 ...

MATHS MICE

Cool School Pets

Miss Flynn's Pangolin

Miss Flynn's pangolin
Hates school dinner
And Miss Flynn's pangolin
Is growing thinner!
Miss Flynn's pangolin
Can't cope with stew
But he's mad about ants
(Which you don't have to chew)
So if Miss Flynn's pangolin
Becomes distressed
Send Miss Flynn to find him
A nice ants' nest!

Sue Cowling

The Fate of the School Hamster

The cat ate it
No, the dog chased it
No, I left it in the garden
And a bird flew off with it
No, a robber stole it
No, a badger made a hole with it
I can't find that hamster, strange isn't it?

An elephant sat on it
No, my aunty flattened it
No, my dad swatted it
No, the rat got it
No, it got squashed by the telly
No, it got squeezed by Kelly
I can't find that hamster, strange, isn't it?

A fire burned it
No, a fan turned it
No, a guitar plucked it
No, a hen clucked at it
No, a snake hissed at it
No, a chopper just missed it
So can we buy a rat, and that be the end of that?

Katie Dale (8)

from ... Me Memba Wen

Me memba wen we use to be ena 4H club
  a school
We use to get bees, pigs, rabbit, fowl, goat,
An all dem tings de fe look after,
One day, more dan all
We a look after de bees, so we tek out
Some honey fe eat,
One a dem bwoy no mek sure im
Smoke off all de bees,
Im bite de honey comb wid bees pon da
De bees bite im ina in mout
Im bawl out WOH, WOH, mi mout, mi mout
An spit out de whole a it.

Frederick Williams

Subtraction

Our French teacher keeps snails,
But we get quite suspicious
When she tells us that keeping snails
Is simply "so delicious!"

She also keeps pet frogs,
She says they're good for kissing,
But what we really want to know
Is why their legs are missing!

Coral Rumble

Cool School Pets

We like grizzly bears and pythons
Alligators, sewer rats.
We like Komodo dragons
And giant vampire bats.
We like man-eating tigers
And tarantulas are nice
But what are we allowed to keep?
Gerbils, goldfish, mice.

Philip Waddell

Teacher's Pet

The teachers in my school must think
they're working in a zoo.
Their classrooms feature many a creature.
Here are just a few:

Mr Lee has a chimpanzee.
It leaps about and wriggles.
It pulls his hair and bumps his chair
and gives us all the giggles.

Mrs Drake has a ten-foot snake
inside a case of glass.
When children shout she lets it out
to quieten down the class.

Mr Matt has a vampire bat
with teeth that smile and bite.
When it's time for sums it shows its gums
and helps us get them right!

Mrs Rider wears a spider
dangling from one ear.
It does no harm. It's meant to charm,
but fills us full of fear.

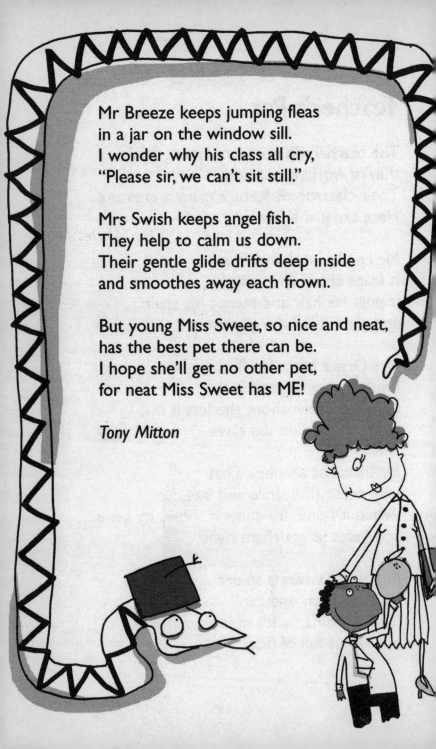

Mr Breeze keeps jumping fleas
in a jar on the window sill.
I wonder why his class all cry,
"Please sir, we can't sit still."

Mrs Swish keeps angel fish.
They help to calm us down.
Their gentle glide drifts deep inside
and smoothes away each frown.

But young Miss Sweet, so nice and neat,
has the best pet there can be.
I hope she'll get no other pet,
for neat Miss Sweet has ME!

Tony Mitton

Haiku

Our budgerigar
Happy to feed on bird seed
Longs for mimosa.

David Whitehead

My Iguana Loves Banana

Puppy and the Sausage

He thinks that it's fighting back
When it burns his nose;
He prances all about it
Barking, making shows.

He snaps at it, but it's too hot;
Tosses it up high,
Then stops to sniff and study it
Pawing nervously.

Now suddenly, the burning cooled,
Here comes the last attack;
He grabs it in his baby teeth
And gulps the sausage back.

Gabriel Fitzmaurice

Dog Byte

When they wish me "Nighty-night"
I look bleary-eyed and gormless –
But this is just a SHAM!
As soon as they're asleep
I'm into my RAM mode!
You've heard of Pack Dogs?
Well, I'm a HACK Dog!
I wonder what they'd do
If half the neighbourhood's
Dog owners knew
Their pets have learned to use
Their owners' computers, late at night?
(We find them useful
For storing information,
Just as humans do.)

Months ago, I opened a window of my own
For where I'd buried things,
Like bones or balls.
But now that I've become a HACKER,
It's even more exciting!
I tap into the records of *other* computers
And find dog-run windows
That list the whens and wheres
Of *their* buried treasures,
Soon to become my own. . .

"A chicken carcass in the vegetable patch"
"A tasty lamb's leg at Number 4"
"Some spare ribs under the apple tree" –
Things they've been saving for a "private gnaw",
Until I dig them up – and "relocate" ...
I'm building quite a collection!
And, joy of joys, no one suspects!
I've avoided all detection,
Thanks to my technological skills.

For I'm a "New-Age" Retriever –
And the results are simply GOLDEN!

Trevor Harvey

Stegosaurus

I have a stegosaurus.
He's really rather sweet.
But he's very, very fussy
About the food he'll eat.

I offered him a burger,
A plate of egg and chips,
A dish of chicken curry,
But none would pass his lips.

I asked, "What would be tasty?
I'll get it if I can."
He said, "I'd better tell you,
I'm a Vegetarian!"

Wendy Larmont

My Pony

velvety nostrils
nuzzle my pockets for mints
wistfully drooling

Sue Cowling

My Pet Alligator

He crawls through the rooms
He likes to watch TV
And he almost eats everything
If he can
But if he doesn't like the food
He gets very mad
So we give him food he likes
Just to be on
The safe
side.

burp.

Thomas Bull (6)

Hello! How Are You? I Am Fine!

Hello! How are you? I am fine!
is all my dog will say,
he's probably repeated it
a thousand times today.
He doesn't bark his normal bark,
he doesn't even whine,
he only drones the same *Hello!*
How are you? I am fine!

Hello! How are you? I am fine!
his message doesn't change,
it's gotten quite monotonous,
and just a trifle strange.
Hello! How are you? I am fine!
it makes the neighbours stare,
they're unaware that yesterday
he ate my talking bear.

Jack Prelutsky

Hello! How are you..?
I am fine!

Iguana Rap

Beside the sofa sits So-Sophia;
my iguana loves ripe bananas,
she'll rap, rap, rap on my school-skirt lap,
flick out her tongue and when she's done
she'll cruise to sleep in the deep, deep heat
from the lamp inside her tank.

Under the sofa sits So-Sophia;
my iguana hates pet gymkhanas,
she'll nap, nap, nap in the tiny gap,
crawl out with ease for a bit of cheese
then cruise to sleep in the deep, deep heat
from the lamp inside her tank.

Moira Clark

Haiku

Sleeps, eats, plays, eats; sleeps
in my favourite chair. "Grrr!"
Sleeps, eats, plays, eats, sleeps. . .

Mike Johnson

A Shaggy One Would Do

Poem Left Hopefully Lying Around Before Christmas

I do want a dog.
It could be just a small one,
A shaggy one would do,
Or a smooth one or a tall one.
It needn't even be
A go-and-fetch-my-ball one;
In fact I wouldn't mind
An any-kind-at-all one.
I just want a dog.

I don't want a cat,
It would just turn up its snoot;
I don't want a sweater,
A computer or a flute;
What I'm trying to say
Is that what would best suit
(Assuming that anyone
Cares a hoot)
Is a D-O-G.

So that's it: a dog.
I wouldn't mind a Great Dane;
Or try me with a scruffy stray:
You'll find I won't complain.
I promise I'll go walks with it –
Even in the rain.
Now in case you haven't got it clear
I'll put it very plain:
Dog, dog, dog, dog, dog.

Eric Finney

The Invisible Man's Invisible Dog

My invisible dog is not much fun.
I don't know if he's sad or glum.
I don't know if, when I pat his head,
I'm really patting his bum instead.

Brian Patten

My Cocker Spaniel (Bonnie)

I'm admired for my ears. Three cheers.
I'm admired for my paws. Applause.
And if somebody chased the cat,
And if somebody chewed the mat,
And if somebody jumped the wall,
And punctured next-door neighbour's ball,
It wasn't me.

I'm admired for my eyes, surprise.
I'm admired for my smile, worthwhile.
And if somebody went upstairs,
And covered beds in doggy hairs,
And if somebody climbed a seat,
And left the marks of muddy feet,
It wasn't me.

Joanne Brown (12)

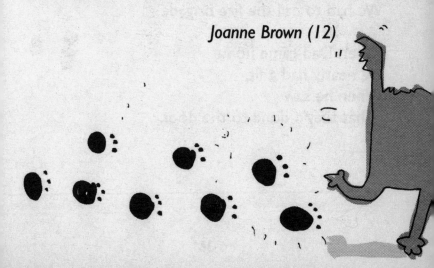

It's a Dog's Life

Mum says
Our dog's
Having an identity crisis.

Yesterday,
He went out into the garden,
Then tried to come back in
Through the cat-flap.

He jammed his head so tight,
No matter how hard
We pushed and pulled
It wouldn't budge.

In the end,
We had to call the fire brigade.

When Dad came home
He nearly had a fit,
When he saw
What they'd done to the door.

He called the dog
All sorts of names.
But when the dog jumped up
To beg for his evening walk,
Dad still took him.

It's not fair.
If I'd smashed the door,
I wouldn't have been allowed out
For at least two weeks!

John Foster

War Dog

Each morning,
before breakfast,
my dog – Chewie Louie,
a shaggy, baggy
hog of a dog,
snatches and catches
his long leathered lead,
daring me to play –
"Tug of War"

Each afternoon,
after school,
my dog – Chewie Louie,
a shaggy, baggy
log of a dog,
batters and splatters me
against the front door,
glaring at me to play –
"Thug of War".

And each evening,
before bed,
my dog – Chewie Louie,
a shaggy, baggy
snog of a dog,
licks and flicks my face
with slobbering tongues of happiness,
declaring, that this time,
he wants to be friends and play –
"Hug of War"!

Ian Souter

Taking the (Shush) For a (Shush)

He understands every word we say,
so we have to be careful.

Shall we take you-know-who
down to the green space with railings round,
to exercise his legs?
I'll find his length of leather
with the clip on the end,
and you fetch his ball —

OH! NO!
What have I said!
DOWN, BOY! DOWN!

Daphne Phillips

Muffin – My Dog

Muffin the mongrel
Has long, droopy ears,
A fringe that covers his eyes,
And a tail like a fan.
He has eyes that shine
In the night.
When I come downstairs
They sparkle – greeny black
Like cat eyes.
He has bits of hair
That stick up – spiky
Like a punk rocker's.
When he opens his mouth,
His tongue hangs out
Between his teeth.
He looks like
He is laughing.

Hayley Morris (7)

My Dog, He is an Ugly Dog

My dog, he is an ugly dog,
he's put together wrong,
his legs are much too short for him,
his ears are much too long.
My dog, he is a scruffy dog,
he's missing clumps of hair,
his face is quite ridiculous,
his tail is scarcely there.

My dog, he is a dingy dog,
his fur is full of fleas,
he sometimes smells like dirty socks,
he sometimes smells like cheese.
My dog, he is a noisy dog,
he's hardly ever still,
he barks at almost anything,
his voice is loud and shrill.

My dog, he is a stupid dog,
his mind is slow and thick,
he's never learned to catch a ball,
he cannot fetch a stick.
My dog, he is a greedy dog,
he eats enough for three,
his belly bulges to the ground,
he is the dog for me.

Jack Prelutsky

Haiku

Behind the cupboard?
Under the stair? We've searched for
that mouse ev'rywhere.

Ann Bonner

Pet Palindrome

A palindrome is a word or a group of words that reads the same forwards and backwards. Can you find the palindrome in the following rhyme?

> You can step on a carpet,
> A rug or a mat,
> And there'll be
> Little cause for regrets;
> But just mind the tortoise
> The dog and the cat.
> I'm telling you:
> Step on no pets!

Eric Finney

Who's Seen Jip?

Jip's run away,
left home for good.
I just *knew* he would,
for earlier today
he was shouted at by dad.
"Bad dog!
Bad dog!
BAD!"

Now Jip's a stray.
What will he eat?
Where will he sleep?
I'm so sad I could weep.
Oh, gloomsday, doomsday,
my dog has gone.

Who's seen Jip?

Anyone?

Wes Magee

Bad Design

A hedgehog misses
children's kisses
their cuddles, coddles, tickles.
Rabbits or mice
seem twice as nice
designed without the prickles.

A nasty, porcupiney skin
will not allow a tickle in –
so tickles, kisses, cuddles, coddles
go to all the furry models.

Jez Alborough

The Cat Sat on the Computer

The cat sat on the computer
It couldn't have been cuter
The cat sat on the computer

The cat sat on the computer
The cat was our cat Mitzi
And she sitzi where she wants to sitzi

The cat sat on the computer
The computer was an Amstrad
The Amstrad of my dad

The cat sat on the computer
The computer swayed like a tree
And the cat sat there contentedly

The cat sat on the computer
One day there was a crash
One day there was a smash

And the computer sat on the cat.

John Whitworth

Marmalade

He's buried in the bushes,
with dock leaves round his grave,
A crimecat desperado
and his name was Marmalade.
He's the cat that caught the pigeon,
that stole the neighbour's meat . . .
and tore the velvet curtains
and stained the satin seat.
He's the cat that spoilt the laundry,
he's the cat that spilt the stew,
and chased the lady's poodle
and scratched her daughter too.

But –
No more we'll hear his cat-flap,
or scratches at the door,
or see him at the window,
or hear his catnap snore.
So –
Ring his grave with pebbles,
erect a noble sign –
For here lies Mr Marmalade
and Marmalade was MINE.

Peter Dixon

The Great Gerbil Hunt

I've looked on the table,
I've searched through the fridge;
the cheese box is empty
I've felt in each vase!
I've checked under carpets,
beneath the settee,
behind every cushion,
below the TV...

Yes, I'm *sure* that I closed it,
honestly Dad –
I knew if I didn't
you'd *really* be mad!
Yes, I *know* he was safe
when I last saw him, Mum...
Well, I *think* that I'm sure...
Yes, I'm *sure* that I am!

That is ...
I'm sure he'll soon come...

LOOK OUT!
DON'T STEP BACK, MUM!

Judith Nicholls

Haiku

Peter parrot pecks,
picks on my poorly pinkie –
I'll tweak his keen beak

Moira Clark

Turkeys Jus Wanna Play Reggae

Quack, Quack!

We have two ducks. One blue. One black.
And when our blue duck goes "Quack-quack"
our black duck quickly quack-quacks back.
The quacks Blue quacks make her quite a
   quacker
but Black is a quicker quacker-backer.

Dr Seuss

Quack Quack

Quack back

My Parakeet

Anyone see my parakeet, Skeet?
He's small and neat,
he's really sweet,
with his pick-pick beak,
And his turn-back feet.

Skeet, Skeet, I wouldn't tell a lie
You are the green-pearl of my eye.

Grace Nichols

Talking Turkeys!

Be nice to yu turkeys dis christmas
Cos turkeys just wanna hav fun
Turkeys are cool, turkeys are wicked
An every turkey has a Mum.
Be nice to yu turkeys dis christmas,
Don't eat it, keep it alive,
I could be yu mate an not on yu plate
Say, Yo! Turkey I'm on your side.

I got lots of friends who are turkeys
An all of dem fear christmas time,
Dey wanna enjoy it, dey say humans destroyed it
An humans are out of dere mind,
Yeah, I got lots of friends who are turkeys
Dey all have a right to a life,
Not to be caged up an genetically made up
By any farmer an his wife.

Turkeys jus wanna play reggae
Turkey's jus wanna hip-hop
Can yu imagine a nice young turkey saying,
"I cannot wait for de chop"?
Turkeys like getting presents, dey wanna watch
christmas TV,
Turkeys hav brains an turkeys feel pain
In many ways like yu an me.

I once knew a turkey called
Turkey
He said, "Benji explain to me please,
Who put de turkey in christmas
An what happens to christmas trees?"
I said, "I am not too sure turkey
But it's nothing to do wid Christ Mass
Humans get greedy an waste more dan need be
An business men mek loadsa cash."

Be nice to yu turkey dis christmas
Invite dem indoors fe sum greens
Let dem eat cake an let dem partake
In a plate of organic grown beans,
Be nice to yu turkey dis christmas
An spare dem de cut of de knife,
Join Turkeys United an dey'll be delighted
An yu will mek new friends "FOR LIFE".

Benjamin Zephaniah

Barry's Budgie! Beware!

Dave's got a dog the size of a lion
Half-wolf, half-mad, frothing with venom
It chews up policemen and then spits them out
But it's nowt to the bird I'm talking about.

Claire's got a cat as wild as a cheetah
Scratching and hissing, draws blood by the litre
Jumps high walls and hedges, fights wolves on its
    own
But there's one tough budgie it leaves well alone.

Murray my eel has teeth like a shark
Don't mess with Murray, he'll zap out a spark
But when Barry's budgie flies over the houses
Murray dips down his lights, blows his own fuses.

This budgie's fierce, a scar down its cheek
Tattoos on its wings, a knife in its beak
Squawks wicked words does things scarcely legal
Someone should tell Barry it's really an eagle.

David Harmer

Sergeant Brown's Parrot

Many policemen wear upon their shoulders
Cunning little radios. To pass away the time
They talk about the traffic to them, listen to the
   news,
And it helps them to Keep Down Crime

But Sergeant Brown, he wears upon his shoulder
A tall green parrot as he's walking up and down
And all the parrot says is "Who's a-pretty-boy-
   then?"
"I am," says Sergeant Brown.

Kit Wright

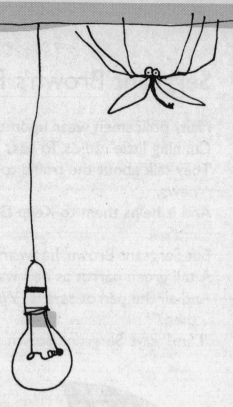

Daddy-Long-Legs

My crane fly is known just as *Goon*
and lurches in each afternoon.
He's not so appealing ...
splays legs on the ceiling
like a space module gripping the moon!

Judith Nicholls

Haiku

Sad eyes. Twitching legs.
He looks so lost and afraid
On the vet's table.

John Kitching

Hello
little
daisy

Vet Required: Apply Within

At the Vet's

When we took our dog to the vet's
we sat and waited with all sorts of pets.

There were hamsters with headaches
and fish with the flu,
there were rats and bats
and a lame kangaroo.

There were porcupines
with spines that were bent
and a poodle that must have been
sprinkled with scent.

There were dogs that were feeling
terribly grumpy
and monkeys with mumps looking
awfully lumpy.

There were rabbits with rashes
and foxes with fleas,
there were thin mice in need of
a large wedge of cheese.

There were cats complaining
of painful sore throats,
there were gerbils and geese
and two travel-sick goats.

There were two chimpanzees
who both had toothache,
and the thought of the vet
made everyone **shake!**

Brian Moses

At The Vet's

You think you're top dog?
Lie down! Wait quietly! Here
all pets are equal.

Anne Allinson

Dream Pet

I dreamed I owned a dinosaur,
I kept it as a pet,
He really caused a panic
When I took him to the vet.

I shoved him in the waiting room,
A woman gave a shout,
The dogs all started barking
So I had to take him out.

The dinosaur was so afraid
He hid behind a car.
The vet said, "You're too big to hide,
I know just where you are!"

Before the vet could calm him down
He'd galloped to the park,
His big teeth made a racket
As they chattered in the dark!

Sue Benwell

Respect, Respect Your Cyberpet

I went to the vet
with my cyberpet
but he said,
"Nothing's been invented yet
to detect what makes a cyberpet
feel dejected and rejected
and start to fret —

"But I'd like to bet
that if your pet gets wet,
it will jump on board a jumbo jet
and fly to the sun
to try to forget
that though you know
you love and respect it,
your cyberpet just feels lost and neglected.

"So when you're alone at home
filled up with regret,
I'd like you to take some time and reflect
that a vet can do nothing
for a cyberpet.

"And before you're met with any more debt,
let your pet get connected
to an electronic vet –
you can download one from the Internet!"

D J Ward

Vet Required: Apply Within

My pet is a monster,
a monster is my pet
and one day I decided
that he should see the vet.

The vet said, "What's the problem,
is he off his food?"
I said, "No, his appetite is monstrous,
mega, amazing, you'd. . ."

"Open wide," said the vet.

". . .be shocked at what he guzzles;
cardboard, carpets, cassettes.
He eats absolutely everything,
even . . . oh dear . . . vets!"

Bernard Young

What Asana Wanted For Her Birthday

Please don't get me
a hamster or budgie.
Please don't get me
a goldfish or canary.

Please get me something
a little scary.
Maybe something
a wee bit hairy.

How about a tarantula?
What's wrong with a spider-pet?
If it gets sick of course
I'll take it to scare –
I mean; to see
– the vet.

Grace Nichols

Haiku

Glitter, my goldfish,
Blows bubbles for me – kisses
Round and wet and sweet.

Jenni Sinclair

My Fish Can Ride a Bicycle

The Hopeful Frog

I had a frog whose name was Jim,
I was extremely fond of him.
He turned into a Prince one day,
I shook my head and ran away.

argh!

Daphne Schiller

– Darling

Mary Had a Crocodile

Mary had a crocodile
That ate a child each day;
But interfering people came
And took her pet away.

Hilaire Belloc

My Fish Can Ride a Bicycle

My fish can ride a bicycle,
my fish can climb a tree,
my fish enjoys a glass of milk,
my fish takes naps with me.

My fish can play the clarinet,
my fish can bounce a ball,
my fish is not like other fish,
my fish can't swim at all.

Jack Prelutsky

Ode to a Goldfish

O
Wet
Pet!

Gyles Brandreth

Small Pet Poem

My newt
is
minute.

Mike Johnson

Hello

Haiku

Don't tell anyone
I have a**... The others
are afraid of them.

Ann Bonner

** əsnoɯ

Whiskers Like Spiky Icicles

A Reasonable Rat

I know a really ravishing reason to become your perfectly plausible pet... And yes, that is the end of my tale. No, you really cannot fail. Have you guessed who I am yet? I'm a wriggily, wittily, well-behaved wonder.

Laurelle Rond

Pocket Friends

Having your pets
close by is nice.
In this pocket
I've got two mice,
and in the other
a pink-eyed rat.
The gerbils ride
inside my hat.
I prefer things
not too big,
like this pygmy
guinea-pig ...

but can you get
a kangaroo
that's big enough
to carry you?

Mark Bones

Who Am I?

My first is in guinea pig but not found in mouse.
My second's in elephant and also in louse.
My third is in rabbit. It isn't in cat.
My fourth is in budgie. You'll find it in bat.
My fifth's in iguana. It's absent from lamb.
My last is in lion, but not found in ram.

If you put first things first
You'll know who I am.
I won't need to draw you
A big diagram.

If the answer's not plain yet,
And that's what you feel,
Imagine the scene
As I race round a wheel!

John Kitching

Answer: a gerbil

Rosie Super Rabbit

Rosie my rabbit is super big.
She can run as fast as a jet
And as fast as Concorde.
Her teeth are long and yellow like knives.
She has two at the top and two at the bottom
And her whiskers are like spiky icicles.
Her ears stick up like two fingers.
They have got veins.
They are pink – like lipstick
And so are her eyes.
She has got a sniffy nose.
Her fur is as white and soft as the middle bit of
  bread
(except for the dirty bits on the bottom of her
  feet).
She crunches up dandelion leaves
And sometimes she can fly
(but don't tell anyone).
She lies down on my legs
But she scratches me sometimes.

Alex Coburn (4)

My Rabbit

My rabbit
has funny habits.

When I say sit
he sits.

When he hears me call
he wags
his tail a bit.

When I throw a ball
he grabs it.

What a funny rabbit!

One day in the park
I swore I heard him bark.

John Agard

Have a Gerbil!

We bought our little gerbil
A little walking wheel
And while we watched the telly,
He just loved to make it squeal.

It went round and round and round and round
And round and round and round.
Amazing how a little thing
Can make that piercing sound.

And when he wasn't wheeling
He was trying to eat his cage.
He would climb up in the corner
And chew metal for an age.

Yes he chewed and chewed and chewed and
  chewed
And chewed and chewed and chewed.
We often used to laugh
About his cheeky attitude.

We liked him ever such a lot
But now we've thought it through –
We think he would be happier
If he came to live with you.

Ian Whybrow

Our Cat's Thoughts About How We Could Avoid Scraping Our Knuckles Trying To Get This Blasted Table Through The Kitchen Door

If only you had whiskers
Like the ones we pussies wear,
you might just turn that sideways
Then you wouldn't have to swear.

Ian Whybrow

Haiku

My cat has a bell
so birds are warned she's coming.
She comes with music.

Philip Burton

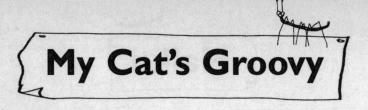

My Cat's Groovy

I Had a Little Cat

I had a little cat called Tim Tom Tay,
I took him to town on market day,
I combed his whiskers, I brushed his tail,
I wrote on a label, "Cat for Sale.
Knows how to deal with rats and mice.
Two pounds fifty. Bargain price."

But when the people came to buy
I saw such a look in Tim Tom's eye
That it was clear as clear could be
I couldn't sell Tim for a fortune's fee.
I was shamed and sorry, I'll tell you plain,
And I took home Tim Tom Tay again.

Charles Causley

My Cat

My cat
got fatter
and fatter.
I didn't know
what was the matter.
Then,
know what she did?
She went into the cupboard
and hid.

She was fat when she went in,
but she came out
thin.
I had a peep.
Know what I saw?
Little kittens
all in a heap –
1 – 2 – 3 – 4.

My cat's great.

Nigel Gray

Cat

My cat is black as darkest night
When no moon rides.
His eyes are green as starlit pools
And midnight tides.

But whenever the day is warm and sunny
His eyes are gold and clear as honey.
He rolls on his back and very soon
His coat is dusty with afternoon.

Ann Bonner

Animal Rights

Our cat
Won't use the cat-flap
Any more.
He's started to fight
For his Animal Rights
And insists
That he uses the door.

Lindsay MacRae

My Cat's Groovy

My cat's groovy
Real choosy,
Thinks the sun's dumb,
Afternoons
He should be snoozing
On the shed roof
But when it hots up
He gets up
And zooms in
Out of the blue
For a quick kip.

But at night
The cat flap flips
And out he slips,
Moves smoothly
Over leaves and roots,
Shoots up the shed roof,
Grooms ears and neck,
Broods,
Lazily eyes his territory
Then lies back
And moonbathes.

My cat's groovy
Dead choosy,
In fact
He's quite
A cool cat.

Gina Claye

My Lovely Pussy Cat

We have a cat her name is Lizzy
Her games make me fairly dizzy.
She licks, she purrs, she sits and begs
And plays with my mum's pegs.
When she scratches at the door
You would think she's not been fed before.
She even rides upon my swing
And doesn't seem to fear a thing.
Now she's curled up fast asleep,
Is she really counting sheep?
No, she's not. She's counting mice,
My pussy cat's life is rather nice.

Joanne Mathieson (7)

Haiku

My cat slinks, black-backed
Through the dark streets of midnight.
His name is Shadow.

Jennifer Curry

What Shall We Call Him?

Our Dog Smartie

Our dog looks like a tube on legs
and he's ever so sweet
so we call him Smartie!
He's a blotchy brown and white colour
with huge ears that look like sheepskin mitts
that have been stitched to the side of his head.
And when he starts to run
they seem to be trying to clap
but never quite meet.

Unfortunately Smartie likes and loves to chew
and I mean chew, *everything and anything*:

carpets, curtains, shoes and doors
chairs, kitchens, gardens and floors,
newspapers, fridges, clothes and toys
bedrooms, televisions and even little boys!

And he especially enjoys *legs*:

Legs of beds,
legs of tables,
legs of chairs
and his favourite delicacy – legs of postmen!

But yesterday Smartie became very *unsmartie*!
You see Dad and I were in the attic playing
  snooker
when Dad went to pot the black.
The cue ball scorched across the green felt
and walloped into the black ball
which then slammed it into the pocket!
"Yes," shouts Dad, "I win!"
"Oh no," whispers me, "you don't!"
For the ball doesn't stop there,
it explodes out of the hole,
and flies across the room –
ZZZZZZZZZOOOOOOMMMMM –
crashing into one of Mum's newly framed pictures!

Guess who had gone and chewed the pockets?

  But guess who Mum chewed up later!

                          Ian Souter

Four Crazy Pets

I've four crazy pets, all rather jolly –
Rover, Tiddles, Flopsy and Polly.
A dog, a rabbit, a parrot and a cat.
Which one's which? Can you guess that?

Rover's a dog? No!
Tiddles is a cat? No!
Flopsy's a rabbit? No!
Polly's a parrot? No!

My dog has the appetite of a small gorilla.
We called her Polly 'cause we can never fill her.

The rabbit has a habit of wetting where we're
    standing.
We call him Tiddles 'cause the puddles keep
    expanding.

Our cat purrs like an engine turning over
Vroom vroom vroom – so we call her Rover.

The fact that our parrot cannot fly is such a shame.
Flopsy by nature and Flopsy by name.

Four crazy names! Wouldn't you agree?
I think my pets fit their names purrfectly.

Paul Cookson

A Parrot Called Mouse

My Grandad has a parrot living in his house –
it talks with a squeak, so he calls it Mouse.
Its feathers flutter with a glitter of blue and
   gold.
It's quite cheeky even though it's quite old.
Grandad grumbles and grunts when it's time for
   bed –
he knows old Mouse has other ideas instead:
with its bold beak it shrieks as it flies free

"Can't catch
   me"

   "Can't catch
      me"

      "Can't catch
         me"

Tim Pointon

What Shall We Call the Dog?

What shall we call our new dog?
He's got to have a name.
Roger? Rover? Rufus? Rex?
No, all of those sound tame.
What shall we call him then?
Come on, it's got to sound just right.
Marcus? Martin? Marlow? Max?
No, none of those fits him quite.
For days the question still remained:
What *shall* we call the dog?
Tanga? Thomas? Tarquin? Terry?
Taurus? Tarzan? Trog?
No, those won't do. What shall it be?
Benedict? Brown? Brunel?
No, we simply call him *Whatshall* –
And he likes it very well.

Eric Finney

Cat

My cat has got no name,
We simply call him Cat;
He doesn't seem to blame
Anyone for that.

For he is not like us
Who often, I'm afraid,
Kick up quite a fuss
If *our* names are mislaid.

As if, without a name,
We'd be no longer there
But like a tiny flame
Vanish in bright air.

My pet, he doesn't care
About such things as that:
Black buzz and golden stare
Require no name but Cat.

Vernon Scannel

Haiku

Can you believe it?
An *elephant* for Christmas!
Dad must be joking!

John Kitching

A Python in the Pantry

Wild Thing

I caught
a caterpillar
Kept it in a jar
to be my pet.

But I had to let it go
soaring to the sky,
too beautiful by far
to keep, when it
became a butterfly.

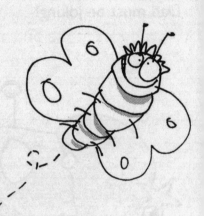

Ann Bonner

Our Hippopotamus

We thought a lively pet to keep
Might be a hippopotamus.
Now see him sitting in a heap,
And notice at the bottom – us.

Colin West

Ernie – the Great Collector

"Exotic Ernie" keeps the oddest creatures,
Anything that's wriggly, scaly, slick.
The neighbours think he's dangerous and dotty
But collecting reptiles gives him a real kick.

There's a salamander snoozing in the cellar
A python in the pantry he calls Pru
Tadpoles in the teapot
Two toads in the bread tin
And a lizard licking
Limescale from the loo.

One lump or 2?

There's a slow worm sucking "Mintoes" on the
    sofa
And eight iguanas on the garage wall
A tortoise on the telly
And a dead frog in the fridge
Who's waiting till
The undertaker calls.

Now Mrs Ernie says she's going to leave him,
She says she needs more space in which to
    spread.
"You always were a fusspot," Ernie mutters.
"I *like* an alligator in the bed."

Patricia Leighton

My Stick Insect is Hiding

w q n s z n t l r u y p m b n a v i s h i d i n g j u s t h e r e

o l i g c

t
c
e
s
n b w e r f x c d h k e z
i
k
c
i
t
s
y
m

d s b z m g h
t f k y

Coral Rumble

Our Car Pet

It runs under the bonnet
And sleeps under the floor
And though I've never seen it
I know it's there for sure.

It drinks screen-washer water
'Cos pet trolls never shirk
And running on the fan belt,
Dad says, is thirsty work.

Dad says it sups at midnight
When all's quiet as the tomb,
The tube down from the filler cap
Supplies its dining room.

Its diet is expensive
Which the feeding stations sell
(Pet trolleum is what trolls like),
Extracted from some shell.

My brother says I'm barmy,
He says dad has me on,
we haven't got a car pet,
The pet troll thing's a con!

But I know dad's not fooling,
I've heard our pet troll's ROAR
And been to pet troll stations
That's why I'm certain sure.

Philip Waddell

Luv Song

I am in luv wid a hedgehog
I've never felt dis way before
I have luv fe dis hedgehog
And everyday I luv her more an more,
She lives by de shed
Where weeds an roses bed
An I just want de world to know
She makes me glow.

I am in luv wid a hedgehog
She's making me hair stand on edge,
So in luv wid dis hedgehog
An her friends
Who all live in de hedge
She visits me late
An eats off Danny's plate
But Danny's a cool tabby cat
He leaves it at dat.

I am in luv wid a hedgehog
She's gone away so I must wait
But I do miss my hedgehog
Everytime she goes to hibernate.

Benjamin Zephaniah

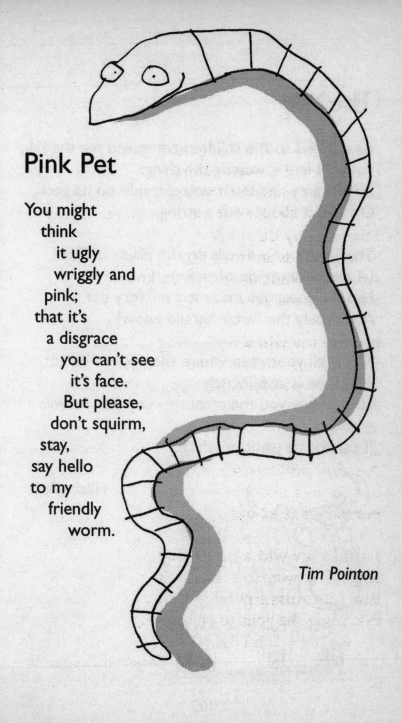

Pink Pet

You might
  think
    it ugly
     wriggly and
  pink;
that it's
  a disgrace
    you can't see
    it's face.
  But please,
  don't squirm,
stay,
say hello
to my
  friendly
    worm.

Tim Pointon

The Yak

As a friend to the children commend me the Yak.
You will find it exactly the thing:
It will carry and fetch, you can ride on its back,
Or lead it about with a string.

The Tartar who dwells on the plains of Tibet
(A desolate region of snow)
Has for centuries made it a nursery pet,
And surely the Tartar should know!

Then tell your papa where the Yak can be got,
And if he is awfully rich
He will buy you the creature – or else he will
   not.
(I cannot be positive which.)

Hilaire Belloc

My Pet Mouse

I have a friendly little mouse,
He is my special pet.
I keep him safely on a lead.
I haven't lost him yet.

I never need to feed him,
Not even bits of cheese.
He's never chased by any cat
And he does just as I please.

He likes it when I stroke him
for he's smooth and grey and fat.
He helps me sometimes with my games,
When he runs around my mat.

I've never ever known a mouse
That could really be much cuter.
He's my extra special 'lectric mouse
That works my home computer.

David Whitehead

Guess the Pet

(A silly riddle)

This pet can't be led
Or be kept in a shed.
This pet is no mouse
It's the size of a house!

This pet's out all weathers
And though it lacks feathers
Does have kinds of scales,
And stands behind rails.

When given a groom
This pet gets the broom
And the bucket and mop. . .
And that's where I'll stop!

Philip Waddell

The silly answer: a pet shop

Auntie Babs

Auntie Babs became besotted
With her snake, so nicely spotted,
Unaware that pets so mottled
Like to leave their keepers throttled.

Colin West

Last Word

A Pet Is...

A pet is a creature
with nothing to do,
its food and shelter
provided by you.

It might be a cat
(with a life of its own)
or a dog, or a horse
(less happy alone).

Or maybe a goldfish,
stick insect, white mouse,
a bird or a snake
has its home in your house.

It really depends
on the time and the space
you can devote
to your pet, in your place.

A tiger or hippo,
a whale or raccoon
are less likely lodgers
in any spare room.

A pet is a creature
with nothing to do
since its life and its living
depend on – just you.

Jane Whittle

Acknowledgements

The compiler and publishers would like to thank the following for permission to use copyright material in this collection. The publishers have made every effort to contact the copyright holders but there are a few cases where it has not been possible to do so. We would be grateful to hear from anyone who can enable us to contact them so that the omission can be corrected at the first opportunity.

John Agard for "My Rabbit" by kind permission of John Agard c/o Caroline Sheldon Literary Agency from *Another Day on My Foot and I Would Have Died*.

Jez Alborough for "Bad Design".

Anne Allinson for "At the Vet's".

Hilaire Belloc for "The Yak". Reprinted by permission of PFD on behalf of: The Estate of Hilaire Belloc, copyright as printed in the original volume. And for "Mary Had a Crocodile".

Sue Benwell for "Dream Pet".

Mark Bones for "Pocket Friends".

Ann Bonner for "Behind the Cupboard", "Don't Tell Anyone" and "Wild Thing". And for "Cat" from *Pussy Cat, Pussy Cat*, ed. Helen Cook & Morag Styles, pub. Cambridge University Press.

Gyles Brandreth for "Ode to a Goldfish".

Joanne Brown for "My Cocker Spaniel" from *Wondercrump Poetry* pub. by Red Fox, copyright Random House Children's Books.

Liz Brownlee for "Purrfect".

Thomas Bull for "My Pet Alligator" from *Wondercrump Poetry* pub. by Red Fox, copyright Random House Children's Books.

Philip Burton for "My Cat Has a Bell".

Charles Causley for "I Had a Little Cat" from *Selected Poems for Children*, pub. Macmillan.

Moira Clark for "Iguana Rap" and "Peter Parrot Pecks".

Gina Claye for "My Cat's Groovy".

Alex Coburn for "Rosie Super Rabbit" from *Wondercrump Poetry* pub. by Red Fox, copyright Random House Children's Books.

Paul Cookson for "Four Crazy Pets" from *A Twist in the Tale*. First published in *Sing That Joke* by Paternoster Publishing, 1998.

Sue Cowling for "Miss Flynn's Pangolin" and "My Pony".

Katie Dale for "The Fate of the School Hamster" © Turning Heads Theatre & Poetry.

Peter Dixon for "Marmalade". First published in *Grow Your Own Poems* pub. Macmillan Education Ltd, 1988.

Eric Finney for "Poem Left Hopefully Lying Around Before Christmas", "Pet Palindrome" and "What Shall We Call the Dog?".

Gabriel Fitzmaurice for "Puppy and the Sausage" from *Puppy and the Sausage*, published by permission of Poolbeg Press, Dublin.

John Foster for "It's a Dog's Life" from *Standing On The Sidelines* by John Foster, pub. OUP 1995, included by permission of the author.

Nigel Gray for "My Cat".

David Harmer for "Barry's Budgie! Beware!".

Trevor Harvey for "Dog Byte". First published in *Techno Talk* compiled by Trevor Harvey, pub. Bodley Head 1994.

Jennifer Curry for "When Lessons Get Dull" and "My Cat Slinks", and also "Glitter My Goldfish" by Jenni Sinclair.

Mike Johnson for "Sleeps, Eats, Plays" and "Small Pet Poem".

John Kitching for "Sad Eyes", "Who am I?" and "Can You Believe It?".

Wendy Larmont for "Stegosaurus".

Patricia Leighton for "Ernie – The Great Collector".

Lindsay MacRae for "Animal Rights". Reproduced by permission of The Agency (London) Ltd © Lindsay MacRae 1995. First published in *Yer Canny Shove Yer Granny Off The Bus* by Viking.

Wes Magee for "Who's Seen Jip?".

Joanne Mathieson for "My Lovely Pussy Cat" © Turning Heads Theatre & Poetry.

Tony Mitton for "Teacher's Pet". First published in *Teacher's Pets*, edited by Paul Cookson, pub. Macmillan, 1999.

Hayley Morris for "Muffin My Dog" © Turning Heads Theatre & Poetry.

Brian Moses for "At the Vet's". First published in *I Wish I Could Dine With A Porcupine* by Brian Moses, pub. Hodder Wayland.

Judith Nicholls for "Daddy Long-Legs". And for "The Great Gerbil Hunt" from *Higgledy Humbug!* by Judith Nicholls, pub. by Mary Glasgow Publications, 1990, reprinted by permission of the author.

Grace Nichols for "My Parakeet" from *No Hickory No Dickory No Dock* and "What Asana Wanted" from *Asana and the Animals*. Reproduced with permission of Curtis Brown Ltd, London. Copyright © Grace Nichols, 1988.

Brian Patten for "The Invisible Man's Invisible Dog" from *Thawing Frozen Frogs*. Reproduced by permission of the author c/o Rogers, Coleridge & White Ltd, 20 Powis Mews, London W11 1JN. Copyright © Brian Patten, 1990.

Daphne Phillips for "Taking the (Shush) for a (Shush)".

Tim Pointon for "A Parrot Called Mouse" and "Pink Pet".

Jack Prelutsky for "Hello! How Are You? I am Fine!" and "My Fish Can Ride a Bicycle" from *Something Big Has Been Here*, text copyright © 1990 by Jack Prelutsky, used by permission of HarperCollins Publishers and "My Dog, He is an Ugly Dog" from *New Kid On The Block* © Jack Prelutsky 1984. Published in the UK by Heinemann Young Books, an imprint of Egmont Children's

Books Limited, London and used with permission.

Laurelle Rond for "A Reasonable Rat".

Coral Rumble for "Subtraction", first published in *Teacher's Pets*, edited by Paul Cookson, pub. Macmillan 1999. And for "Stick Insect" and "Pet Shop Rap".

Vernon Scannel for "Cat".

Daphne Schiller for "The Hopeful Frog".

Dr Seuss for "Quack, Quack!" from *Oh Say Can You Say?* © Dr Seuss Enterprises, L.P. 1979. All rights reserved. Used by permission.

Ian Souter for "War Dog" and "Our Dog Smartie".

Philip Waddell for "Cool School Pets", "Our Car Pet" and "Guess the Pet".

D J Ward for "Respect, Respect, Your Cyberpet".

Colin West for "Our Hippopotamus" and "Auntie Babs".

David Whitehead for "Our Budgerigar" and "Our Pet Mouse".

Jane Whittle for "A Pet Is".

John Whitworth for "The Cat Sat on the Computer" from *The Complete Poetical Works of Phoebe Flood*, by John Whitworth, reproduced by permission of Hodder & Stoughton Ltd.

Ian Whybrow for "Have a Gerbil" and "Our Cats Thoughts".

Frederick Williams for "Me Memba Wen". (This poet cannot be traced.)

Kit Wright for "Sergeant Brown's Parrot" from *Rabbiting On* by Kit Wright, pub. HarperCollins, by permission of the publisher.

Bernard Young for "Vet Required: Apply Within" from *Brilliant* by Bernard Young, pub. Kingston Press.

Benjamin Zephaniah for "Talking Turkeys" and "Luv Song" from *Talking Turkeys*, pub. Viking, 1994. Copyright © Benjamin Zephaniah 1994.